LOVE EQUALS
Sacrifice

AF344280

LOVE EQUALS *Sacrifice*

THE JOURNEY OF LOYALTY AND SERVICE

Michael Stidham

Tate Publishing & Enterprises

Love Equals Sacrifice
Copyright © 2008 by Michael Stidham All rights reserved.

This title is also available as a Tate Out Loud product. Visit www.tatepublishing.com for more information.

No part of this publication may be reproduced, stored in a retrieval system or transmitted in any way by any means, electronic, mechanical, photocopy, recording or otherwise without the prior permission of the author except as provided by USA copyright law.

The opinions expressed by the author are not necessarily those of Tate Publishing, LLC.

Published by Tate Publishing & Enterprises, LLC
127 E. Trade Center Terrace | Mustang, Oklahoma 73064 USA
1.888.361.9473 | www.tatepublishing.com

Tate Publishing is committed to excellence in the publishing industry. The company reflects the philosophy established by the founders, based on Psalm 68:11,
"The Lord gave the word and great was the company of those who published it."

Book design copyright © 2008 by Tate Publishing, LLC. All rights reserved.
Cover and Interior design by Kandi Evans

Published in the United States of America

ISBN: 978-1-60799-141-0
1. Family & Relationships / Aging
09.12.02

To my family and friends.
Thanks for everything.

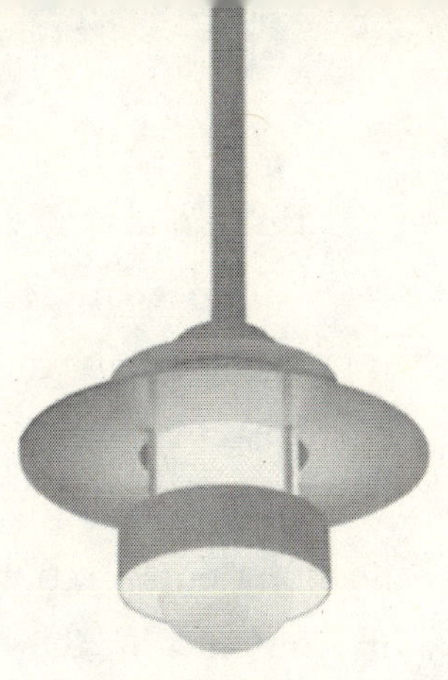

FOREWORD

First, let me say that I'm honored Mike has chosen me to have a small part in this endeavor. Having known him for roughly twenty-five years, I am proud and privileged to call him a lifelong friend.

This story describes a journey that all of us can relate to at one time or another. It's a story of life and death, and the meaning found within. It touches on loyalty, love, and service to fellow man. It made me rethink the way I look at life, concerning my wants and needs, and what is really important in the grand scheme of things.

I'm currently a registered nurse working with America's elderly veterans. In the past, I've also worked with cancer patients and their families. Reading this story and dealing with end of life issues over my career have opened my eyes to what is truly important.

I'm currently married, with two children, and occasionally help out my elderly parents. After reading this story, I found myself thinking, *Man, you really hit the nail on the head. It's in giving that you also receive.* I was inspired and found myself with a sense of renewal. I wanted to immediately share this story with my family and friends. My hope is that everyone reading this will also find a sense of renewal, satisfaction, and revelation that Mike has encompassed so well.

David K. Grome, RN
Southgate, Kentucky
August, 2008

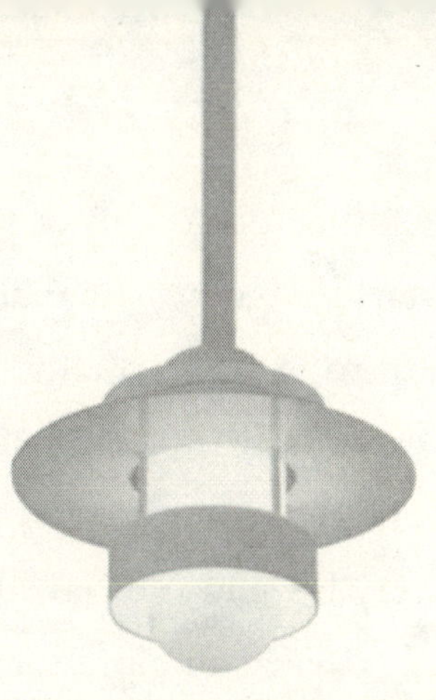

My Parents, Harold and Martha

Love equals sacrifice. Amazingly it took me over forty years to figure this out.

My father, Harold, was born in January of 1925, in Hazard, Kentucky. He was one of five children with two brothers and two sisters. While he was very young, his parents purchased a house, and they moved to Northern Kentucky. During the 1930s, his father passed away suddenly, and his mother started having financial problems. She couldn't afford to support all five of her children and was eventually forced to put Harold and his two brothers in a home for boys. He and his brothers had very little in the way of possessions. They each had two sets of clothes and were only allowed to shower once a week. For Easter each of them received one orange and for Christmas, one apple. Not much of a childhood by today's standards.

Like most men in their late teens, Harold was drafted into the army during World War II. Understandably, he didn't say much about his experiences in Europe, but what he did tell me was very interesting.

Soon after he was drafted, Harold boarded a ship that sailed for England. He said, "That was one rough voyage." For most of the men, it was their first time on a ship, and the sea was not cooperating. Just about everyone was seasick. For most of the war, Harold was stationed in France and served as his squad's medic. Looking at the photos he brought back is almost like watching an episode of *Combat* on television.

Among other things, each month Harold received two cartons of cigarettes. He didn't smoke, and where they were located, American cigarettes were just as valuable as gold. Harold did trade them for a few items here and there, but most of the time, he gave his cigarettes to his friends.

Later in the war, Harold worked at an army hospital. I'm sure it wasn't very funny to his patients, but Harold and his co-workers would occasionally get a ten-inch syringe and walk into the hospital ward. One of them would hold up the syringe, look around, and ask, "Where is Sergeant Myers?" Harold said, "You should have seen the look on his face when he saw that needle." It was just their idea of a little joke. I'm sure Harold and the people he worked with had to keep their spirits up somehow.

After the war was over in Europe, Harold and his friends remained there and were being retrained. They were preparing to ship out to the Pacific and fight the Japanese. Needless to say, they weren't very happy about that. Prior to them shipping out, the two atomic bombs were dropped in Japan, and the war was over. They were so relieved that they'd be heading back home. Thankfully, Harold made it through the war without being injured. One of the first things he told my mother after they were married was, "Don't ever serve me Spam for dinner." Apparently, for several weeks at a time, that's all the army provided.

After being discharged from the army, Harold worked several years at a local hardware chain. He was always very handy around the house and could handle most medium-sized construction projects. Over time, he put a lot of effort into improving our home.

Up until he retired in February of 1987, Harold worked nearly thirty years as a salesman for a toy and home products wholesaler. Back at that time, most retailers didn't buy directly from the manufacturers. This was the perfect job for his personality. Harold got along with just about everyone he met. Our family often accused him of "running for office" every time he would strike up a conversation with a total stranger. When we were younger, his job worked out very well for my brothers, sisters, and me. Each year, with a limited supply going to the public, Harold could always get his hands on the hard-to-find toys for Christmas.

My mother, Martha, was born in January of 1926. While growing up, she lived in Bellevue, Kentucky, which is a few miles south of

Cincinnati, Ohio. She was the oldest of three children in a middle class family. Martha and her two sisters, Joan and Eileen, were all raised in the Catholic faith. They attended a Catholic grade school, which was affiliated with their church, St. Anthony. After graduating from high school, Martha went on to nursing school and eventually became a registered nurse.

While Harold was in high school, he earned some money helping out an elderly man in Bellevue. On Sundays, Harold would take him to church at St. Anthony. That's where he met my mother for the first time. After that, Harold regularly attended mass just to see her. Following several years of dating, he and my mother were married at St. Anthony in May of 1948.

Martha and her cousin, Pauline, were about the same age. Both of them were married and raising a family in Northern Kentucky. Over time, Martha had five children, and Pauline had four.

Throughout her marriage, Martha would be a little nervous each time she found out Pauline was pregnant. Usually within six months, Martha was next. It was kind of a running joke in our family. In her late thirties, while Pauline was pregnant with her fourth child, Martha was thinking, *oh no!* Of course, two months later, she was pregnant with me.

My oldest brother's name is also Harold. Next in line is my sister, Susan. Dave is the middle child, and my sister, Nancy, was born next. I am the last of five children. Martha spent her entire career at the same Salvation Army Hospital. While we were growing up, she worked part-time on second shift. Martha would take care of us during the day, and my father would take over when he arrived home from work at about five o'clock in the evening. At that time a family could get by reasonably well with only one parent working. My parents, however, felt more comfortable with the extra income. Among other things, they used it for our education and our family vacations to Florida each summer. Like most parents, Harold especially tried to give us the childhood he never had.

Throughout the years, our family celebrated most of the major holidays together, and my parents were always very good to us at Christmas. During the fall of 1978, my brothers, sisters, and I wanted to try and repay our parents for their generosity over the years. Martha had always dreamed of going to Hawaii, so we decided to surprise them at our Christmas Eve party with a ten-day trip. I was only twelve at the time, but eventually I saved up seventy-five dollars to contribute. Martha was very emotional when she unwrapped the box and saw the plane tickets and brochure. I remember this as one of her happiest moments.

When the five of us were old enough, Martha

transferred to first shift at the hospital and worked full time up until she retired in February of 1988. After retiring, she spent most of her time reading and traveling. She would go to the library on Monday, check out three books, and return the next Monday for three more. Martha and her sisters would often go on trips to historic sites in our area. My parents also did a lot of traveling throughout the U.S., mostly on bus tours. They would return from one trip, and my mother would literally sign them up for their next one within twenty-four hours.

Harold and Martha were always proud of the fact that all five of their children graduated from college. Three of us went on to teaching careers, and two of us gravitated toward a career in business.

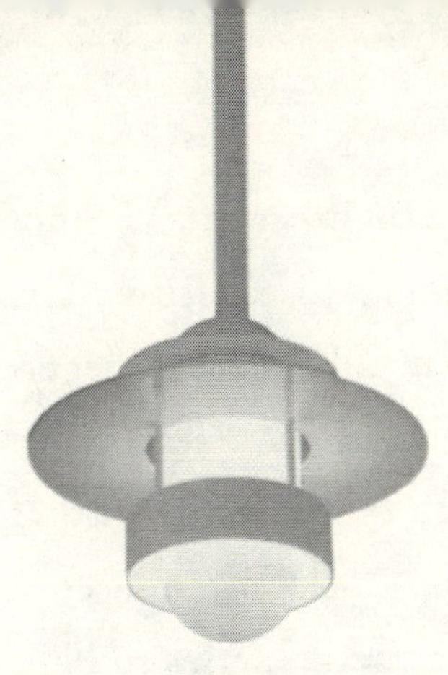

Growing Up and Searching for a Career

My parents, along with my four brothers and sisters, moved back to Bellevue, Kentucky, in February of 1959. Harold wanted to leave Hamilton, Ohio, in order to live closer to his employer. I was born a few years later in December of 1965. My siblings and I went to the Catholic grade school at St. Anthony, the same school my mother attended.

Following the eighth grade, I stopped going to church on Sundays and drifted away from religion somewhat. Like most teenagers, I thought I knew everything. After graduating from Bellevue High School, I attended Northern Kentucky University and majored in accounting. I was always pretty good at math and liked business, so this seemed like the proper direction.

Shortly after graduating from college in May of 1988, I accepted a position with a small CPA firm in the area. There were two partners, and I was one of three accountants. Working in a small firm was beneficial because I was exposed to most facets of accounting. If I chose to work at a larger firm, I would have specialized in only one area.

Despite gaining a lot of experience, the most important thing I learned in my two years at the firm was how *not* to treat your employees. Unfortunately, the two partners were less than diplomatic and did not promote a very happy work environment. I tried my hardest, but nothing seemed to satisfy them. During one conversation with a partner, he was saying something to the effect of, "If you don't start making more money, you'll never be successful." I just looked at him, thinking, *that's how you determine the success of your life?* On one occasion, my relatives noticed there might be an underlying problem when I wasn't even slightly happy about receiving a fifteen percent pay raise. Of the twenty or so employees they went through in a ten-year period, I was there the second longest. A coworker of mine, Denise, had the longest tenure. She left the firm a few months prior to me leaving. In order to receive my CPA certificate, I needed two years of full time experience under a CPA's supervision. Once I had completed that, it was time to move on.

After leaving the CPA firm, I was unemployed for about one year. Going from interview to interview, I was rejected by most of the companies where I applied. One day while browsing through the newspaper, I ran across a *business for sale* ad, namely, a sports bar. With four years of college, I was reasonably familiar with drinking establishments, and with a background in accounting, I decided to take the bull by the horns and go for it. The seven prior owners couldn't make a go of the place, most only lasted about two years.

I had something to prove to myself, and even though it was very hard work, I spent the next twelve years of my life running what turned out to be a very successful business. Every day seemed like a new experience with people occasionally stopping in from far off places like Australia and England. We were one of the few establishments open on Sundays, so the hotels in the area sent their out-of-town clients in our direction. What I learned from people, and especially about them, could have been spread over three lifetimes. I was very fortunate. As well as the good side of people,

I also witnessed the dark things they are capable of. Some of the *fictional things* I've seen on television, I've also witnessed in real life.

At the beginning of my business venture, I gave my parents part ownership in the corporation in exchange for living with them during these years. With finances tight on occasion, it was nice not to worry about a house payment.

When I first arrived, the building was in decent shape, but there were several small projects in need of attention. My background was in accounting, so I didn't have much general construction knowledge. Harold, on the other hand, was retired at this time, and his assistance was very much appreciated. I learned a lot from him over the years and could eventually handle most medium-sized projects, although I never felt very comfortable dealing with electricity. This seemed a little dangerous for me, so I usually called in an electrician for those projects.

Harold was always kind of a clean freak. He showered once a day, was always clean-shaven, and his work clothes were cleaned and pressed. He washed his car at least once a week, and our grass at home was always in pristine condition. It seemed like he and a neighbor of ours were always in a competition for the nicest yard. My business had an area of grass that required cutting, and this was right up Harold's alley. I could have probably cut it in one hour, but it took him about three. It was always well manicured, and Harold enjoyed joking with the customers about me being a slave driver. They would usually ask him if I had given him a raise yet. Harold would usually say I was too cheap or something like that. I just laughed and shook my head. Sometimes this drove my mother crazy. She never understood why Harold and she had to schedule their vacations around grass cutting, but this took priority in his mind.

I usually worked about sixty hours a week, but

life wasn't all work. With Harold being retired, he and I were able to play golf about twice a week. We were pretty good for not playing too often. Harold shot in the low fifties for nine holes, and I usually shot in the low forties. Sometimes it bothered him that I won each time, but I tried to explain that it wasn't a competition. After all, I was forty years younger than he was. Occasionally a stranger, about Harold's age, would join up and play with the two of us. Harold could usually beat him, so he felt better when we were finished.

Harold started playing golf shortly after he retired from work. For his birthday one year, my brothers and I bought him a set of clubs and a pair of golf shoes. I started playing golf during my freshman year in high school. About two years later, I was good enough to join my school's golf team. We are pretty lucky in Northern Kentucky. There are several nice public courses, and when I started golfing, you could play nine holes with a

riding cart for about six dollars. Good luck find-
ing that today.

At first, golfing seemed a little ironic to me.
When I was about eight years old, a friend also
named Mike, and I were in my backyard, playing
with miniature golf clubs. He took a full swing
with the driver, and I was standing just a little
too close. He hit me square in the eye, and I don't
think I've ever screamed that hard in my life. My
mother raced outside, and I ended up in the hospital for about a week with a dislocated retina.
My eyesight eventually returned, but for years I
swore I'd never touch a golf club again. Despite
this incident, he and I remain friends to this day.

If you ever get the chance to go into business
for yourself, please take it. I learned so much during those years. I handled everything from legal
work to marketing, and plumbing to bartending.
Early in life I was always terrified of public speaking, but over time, as I dealt with my vendors and

clients, the fear eventually wore off. I especially enjoyed talking with my clients and learned a lot from them over the years. Throughout my life, I always felt it was okay to make mistakes as long as I didn't repeat them. Sometimes you learn more from your mistakes than you do from your successes. One nice thing about the sports bar was I could listen to other people and learn from their mistakes as well as my own. Every one of my customers had their problems, but it always felt good that they could come in for a little while and have some fun. It was nice to get a paycheck and at the same time provide them with a little happiness.

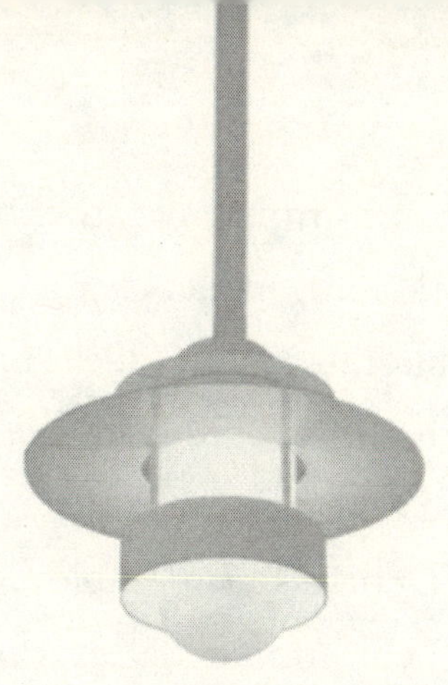

My Oldest Brother

My parents' first child, born in February of 1950, was my brother Harold. During her pregnancy, Martha had this uncontrollable craving for Pepsi. Before my brother was born, my father often asked her how Pepsi was doing, since they didn't have a name for the baby yet. Shortly after his birth, my parents nicknamed him Pep. Over time, to distinguish him from my father, most people called him by his nickname.

Pep and his future wife, Deb, first met during their summer break from college in 1969. My mother helped Pep get a job at the hospital where she worked. Deb was also employed there, and the two of them started dating. Deb's parents were farmers and lived about half an hour away from our house in Bellevue. Deb always laughs about when they were first going out. She went from the dean's list to academic probation in one semester. She said, "It's amazing what falling in love can do."

Deb worked on getting her grades back up and eventually graduated from college in May of 1972. Six weeks later, Pep and Deb were married at St. Anthony's Church in Bellevue. Shortly thereafter, they moved into their first apartment in Lexington, Kentucky. Pep had one more year of college to finish, so Deb found a temporary job as a bookkeeper. During their first years of marriage, they had very little extra money and couldn't afford much in the way of entertainment. Their exciting weekend was being able to afford a two-liter of Pepsi and a twin bag of potato chips. They sat home and watched movies on television. Even as poor as they were back then, it's refreshing to see how Deb treasures those times with Pep.

Shortly after graduating from college, Pep found a teaching position. Deb quit her bookkeeping job in Lexington, and they both moved back to Northern Kentucky. Deb also wanted to teach, so she applied at several schools and eventually found a job ten minutes away from Pep's.

Pep's first and only teaching position was at Bellevue High School. He taught biology and general science, along with his favorite pastime, coaching girl's track and field. Each spring he would spend about two months preparing for and hosting one of Kentucky's largest invitational track meets. Teams came from all over the state, and the events ran on Friday evening and continued all day on Saturday.

During my freshman year at Bellevue High School, I was scheduled to take biology, so I had Pep for a teacher. It was a little strange calling him Mr. Stidham, but we both made it through all right. Over time, I realized that he was one of the most popular teachers in the school. Pep was well liked by the other teachers and the students, especially the girls who ran on his track team. Of course he wanted to win like the other coaches, but he was mainly interested in building up the girls' self-confidence. Whether someone came in first or last, Pep went out of his way to make sure she felt good about what she had accomplished.

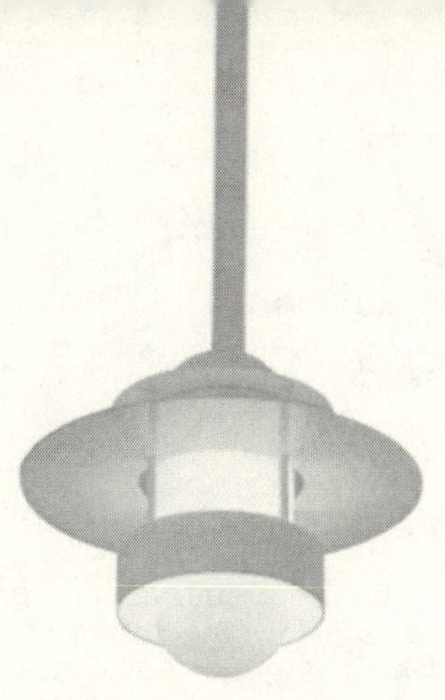

April of 1998

In April of 1998, Pep was hosting the annual Bellevue Invitational Track Meet. Harold and Martha were traveling out west touring several of our national parks. During an afternoon break on Saturday, Pep stopped by my house to get a break from the heat. We talked for a little while, but his schedule was tight, and he had to get back to work. The track meet usually ended pretty late, and Deb wouldn't see him at home until about midnight. He had Sunday to recuperate, and it was back to work, teaching on Monday morning. On my day off, that following Wednesday, our phone rang about nine o'clock in the morning. It was my sister's husband, Bill. At first he didn't sound like his usual self, and then he told me that Pep had passed away. I couldn't believe it! Pep was only forty-eight years old, and everything seemed fine when I was talking to him that prior Saturday. I asked Bill what happened, but he didn't have too many details. All morning it felt like I was having a bad dream and couldn't wake up.

I was in sort of a haze all morning, but eventually I phoned the hotel in San Antonio where my parents were staying. They weren't in at the time, so I left a message for them to call me. Soon after, Martha called back. I asked her to sit down and told her the news. She took it reasonably well and said they would get back home as soon as possible. I can't imagine what it was like to be told your child just passed away. It's just not natural for children to die before their parents.

That afternoon, I wanted to call Deb, but I was too upset. I doubt if I could have even said anything over the phone. Even the principal where Pep worked told me the same thing later that week. Pep was that well liked by the people around him.

After my parents arrived home that Thursday, Deb drove to our house to talk about the funeral arrangements. When I arrived home from work around eight o'clock in the evening, I saw their cars and knew all three of them were in the house. I was afraid to even walk in, but when I eventually did, all three were pretty well composed. Deb told us that Pep went to bed Tuesday night and everything was fine. When she tried to wake him up Wednesday morning for work, he didn't respond. She called 911 right away, but it was too late to do anything. The coroner concluded that Pep died of heart failure while he was sleeping.

St. Anthony is a large church, but it was standing room only for Pep's funeral. Friends of his that I hadn't seen for fifteen years even made an appearance. Also, girls from his prior track teams came to pay their respects. No death is easy to handle, but this was the hardest for me so far. Pep was there one minute, everything seeming all right, and then he was gone the next.

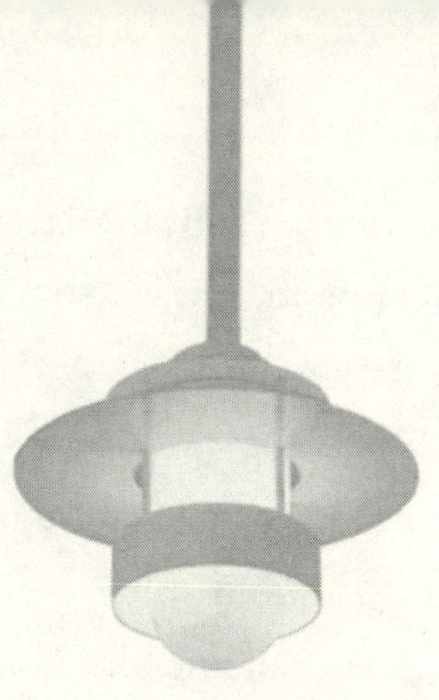

August of 2000 through February 2005

When the weather permitted and she wasn't traveling, Martha enjoyed sitting on our porch and reading. If the weather was bad or it was too dark, she usually read inside on the couch. During August of 2000, I was home one evening, finishing up some paperwork for my business. I walked by the couch, glanced up, and Martha was sitting there reading. About fifteen minutes later, I walked by again and noticed something wasn't right. She sat there motionless, with her eyes and mouth open. My father was upstairs, and I yelled for him to come down. I tried taking her pulse, but felt nothing. Harold came down as quickly as he could. With a horrified look on his face, he took her by the arm and said, "No…no…don't leave me, sweetheart." I will never forget what he said. I felt so sorry for him. I immediately ran to the phone and called 911. Charlie, a longtime neighbor of ours, was on the fire department and heard our address come over his scanner at home. He rushed down a few minutes later to see what the problem was. After he came in, Charlie and I slid Martha onto the floor to perform CPR. A few minutes later, the paramedics arrived and tried several other procedures to revive her. I knew things weren't going very well. As the minutes went by, I noticed the paramedics were in less and less of a hurry. Harold and I followed the ambulance to the hospital, and they put the two of us in a private area near the emergency room. About fifteen minutes later, a doctor came in, and by the look on his face, I knew the news wasn't good. He said he was very sorry, but there was nothing they could do; Martha had passed away. Harold handled the news pretty well at the time. I think we were both in a state of shock. I drove the both us of home, and we just sat in the living room for a while. Eventually we went to bed, but I doubt if either of us got much sleep. This was a crushing blow to my father who was seventy-five at the time. We had lost my brother Pep two years before, and now my mother, his lifelong companion of nearly fifty-three years, was gone.

You may have seen people die on television. They stop moving, and the special effects people change their skin color a bit. This was the first time I had experienced it in real life, and it's somewhat different. At the time, I couldn't explain it. In appearance, it just did not look like my mother. Something was missing.

After Martha passed away, Harold and I talked about going out for dinner once in a while. A few weeks later, on the first Wednesday of the month, Harold; his sister-in-law, Eileen; her cousin, Pauline; and I started going out to a fine dining restaurant. The three of them had lost their spouses over time, so we decided to start up a monthly dinner club. Harold was always a steak-and-potatoes man. He never did drink much, but he did enjoy a whisky sour when we went out for dinner. He was reasonably predictable, so the three of us knew exactly what he was going to order. Whisky sour, shrimp cocktail, filet mignon, medium well, baked potato, and dessert. We enjoyed each other's company and usually spent about three hours at dinner. The girls did most of the talking, but this was normal for our family. Every Sunday, Harold and I would also go out for dinner at a casual restaurant.

Harold was almost a different person in public. He loved talking to people, whether he knew them or not. Occasionally, Harold, Eileen, Pauline, and I would take short day trips to an aquarium, a movie, or Keeneland Race Track. On the way home we'd usually stop off somewhere for dinner. During one trip to the track, Harold and I pooled our money and bet on a long shot. The horse ended up winning, and we split about four hundred dollars. Boy, was Harold happy. Like a kid in a candy store. The three of us tried to get Harold out of the house as much as possible because he always seemed happier.

Juggling a sixty-hour workweek and trying to help out my father, was a lot of work. I didn't like leaving him at home by himself, but at the time there wasn't much I could do. My mother handled the finances for the two of them, along with just about everything else. Among other things, I would wash Harold's clothes once a week. I suppose that's when I first noticed something might be wrong. Over the months ahead, I saw less and less of my father's shirts, pants, and socks in the hamper. This puzzled me because he was always very meticulous about how he looked and dressed. Harold regularly attended church and always showed up in a nice suit and tie. It eventually got to the point where I didn't see any of his clothes in the hamper.

Throughout his life, Harold was always involved in charitable activities, including delivering Meals on Wheels and serving food to the homeless at a local soup kitchen. He also belonged to St. Vincent DePaul and was an officer on St. Anthony's Parish Council. Following my mother's death, he slowly gave up one activity after the other. In hindsight it seems very clear to me now what was going on, but not having a medical background, I really didn't notice the signs back then.

On several occasions, I would come home from work, and Harold would be sitting in his chair with a frustrated look on his face. I'd look at the television, and the picture was all fuzzy. Like a lost, little boy, he would say, "I couldn't get the TV to work." I felt awful that he was sitting there all day with nothing to watch. I told him to call me at work if there was ever a problem, but sometimes he wouldn't.

One afternoon, Harold was walking around the living room, and he appeared to be in pain. I asked what the problem was, and he told me his foot was bothering him for about a week. I took his shoe off and found a callus the size of a small pebble on the bottom of his foot. I shook my head and said, "No wonder your foot hurts; you've basically been walking around on a rock." I used a small battery operated tool and sanded down the callus. You could see the relief on his face when he stood up. I asked, "Why didn't you tell me about this earlier?" He said, "Well, I didn't want to bother you, son." He didn't realize that it was easier on me if I knew he was feeling all right and not in any pain. After that, I started checking his feet on a regular basis.

I tried to walk a fine line in deciding what responsibilities I thought Harold could handle. I didn't want to take away any of his freedom, but I also wanted to make sure he was well cared for and no one was taking advantage of him. In early 2002, I came downstairs one morning on my day off. Walking past the dining room table, I noticed a pamphlet about several types of insurance. I asked Harold where it came from, and he told me a salesman came to our door the prior day. I glanced at the information and put it aside. A little later while paying some of Harold's bills, I noticed one of his checks was missing. I asked him if he used the check, and he said he gave it to the insurance salesman. Harold told the salesman that I took care of paying his bills, but the salesman offered to help Harold write the check. I was furious that someone would take advantage of a seventy-seven-year-old man. The $5,000.00 check was only a down payment for insurance! Fortunately, I caught it in time, and the bank stopped payment on the check. After this incident, I kept Harold's checkbook hidden. Fortunately nothing like this happened in the future.

During August of 2002, after twelve years in business for myself, I decided it was time to sell. I received a decent offer from a competitor, and the timing could not have been better. Shortly after this, Harold started heading downhill. His memory was getting worse, he was losing the ability to speak, and physically he couldn't do much on his own. For the past twenty years, I didn't feel the need for the Catholic Church, but from this point on that was all about to change.

During their retirement years, Harold and Martha traveled a lot on bus trips throughout most of the U.S. They enjoyed the sites and the people they met along the way. They've toured Branson several times and visited most of our national parks. In early 2003, Harold and I decided to take a five-day bus trip to and from New Orleans. It was my first vacation in twelve years and was long overdue. I signed us up with the same tour company that Harold and Martha used out of Louisville. It was the first time I had met my parents' usual tour guide, Marvin, who was also the owner of the company. He was a very nice man about my father's age and made everyone feel welcome on the trip. We toured a good portion of the city, took a cruise on the Mississippi, and ate at several nice restaurants. Our winters in Bellevue were sometimes very cold, so going south where it was in the mid-seventies was a welcome change. One day in New Orleans, Harold and I were eating lunch with a few elderly couples in our group. Harold walked away from the table for something, and a very nice lady leaned over towards me. She said, "I think your father might have Parkinson's. I was a nurse who worked primarily with the elderly, and I've noticed the tremors in his hands." I was startled. His current doctor didn't mention a word about this. I thanked her and said I'd look into it further when we arrived back home. For years Harold had slight tremors in his hands, but I didn't think much of it.

A few months after our New Orleans trip, I accompanied Harold to his next doctor's appointment. We both walked into the treatment room where the doctor was waiting. Prior to this, I had written up a list of concerns I had about Harold's current condition, which the doctor read. I thought I was finally going to get some answers to what was going on. The doctor weighed Harold, took his blood pressure, listened to his heart, and talked to him for a few minutes. Then the doctor turned to me and said, "Well, everything looks okay." I couldn't believe it! My jaw about hit the floor. At this time, Harold was shuffling his feet instead of walking, and getting a one-word answer out of him was doing pretty good. We just paid the bill and left.

Eileen's husband, Bob, who passed away in January of 1991, was self-employed as a doctor. Our family went to him over several decades for most of our medical needs. He was well respected by his patients, and he would never accept payment from our family for his services. We were always very grateful. After he passed away, Eileen, Harold, and Martha changed over to this particular doctor who was a friend of Eileen's. Martha made little comments over time about not being quite satisfied with him, but my parents never did change doctors. This was the first time I had met him, and I began to understand Martha's concerns. This doctor had a long, distinguished career, but he was in his late seventies. It seemed to me that he should think about retiring. With Harold's condition deteriorating, I thought it wise to seek out a younger doctor.

Our first visit with Harold's next doctor was much more productive. The doctor examined him very thoroughly. He took his blood pressure, drew some blood for testing, performed an EKG—basically a full checkup. Near the end of the examination, I expressed my concerns about Harold shuffling his feet and his lack of memory. I told him Harold's current demeanor was nothing like his normal behavior of a few years ago. The doctor observed Harold's shuffling, and most important to me, gave him a memory test. Harold knew his birth date, my name, and some other details. However, when questioned about anything current, like the year or day of the week, Harold was clueless. I estimate he scored about fifty percent. Before deciding on a course of action, the doctor said he wanted to look at the test results when they were completed. We thanked him and set up an appointment for the next month. I was very relieved afterwards and felt this doctor knew what he was doing. Things seemed like they were finally heading in the right direction.

I was very impressed because four hours later, Harold's new doctor phoned our house. He said that Harold's blood sugar was reasonably high. He asked what pharmacy we used and called in a prescription, which I picked up later that evening. After each monthly visit, Harold received one new medication if needed. This way, I could observe any side effects; we knew what medication they were associated with and could make any changes if needed. Over time, Harold did very well on his medication. There was only one we had to change due to a side effect.

Harold remained on his blood sugar pills from that point on. Even though we both liked Coke, cookies, and dessert, I eventually removed them from the house. He would go on little hunting expeditions, so hiding them wasn't an option. Harold always seemed to find them. I felt that if I asked him to do without these things, then it was only fair that I did also. His sugar level could handle a Coke or dessert once in a while, but we only had them when we went out for dinner. As far as his cereal, Splenda worked out well as a substitute for sugar. It tasted pretty good to me, and he didn't notice the difference. Harold eventually adjusted to these changes, and his blood sugar remained reasonably stable. Outside of a little back pain, Harold was always pretty healthy throughout his life. Prior to this, he was fortunate not to be on any prescription medication.

At Harold's next doctor's visit, I wanted to address his memory problems. The doctor talked things over with us and wanted to try Harold on Aricept. This was a once-a-day Alzheimer's drug, which he said would hopefully stop his mental deterioration. It was also supposed to bring him back to the way he was six months prior to his current condition. After a month or so, Harold's memory loss appeared to be stabilizing. Aricept seemed to stop his mental deterioration, and over time his speech and memory began to improve. I was very thankful for this medication. It was expensive, but worth every penny.

Occasionally, Harold would say something awful to me that under normal circumstances would have been very painful. Fifteen minutes later, he was in a good mood and had no idea he'd even said it. Although still difficult, it was a little easier to handle because I knew he was saying things that were basically out of his control.

About a month later, we addressed Harold's blood pressure, which at the time was around 170 over 130. The doctor prescribed medication, but prior to starting Harold on it, I wanted to try and get his blood pressure down by adjusting his diet. Two or three times a week, Harold would have bacon and eggs for breakfast. I was startled at the amount of salt he put on his eggs. He would move the shaker for about five seconds. Over the next week, I removed all the saltshakers from the house. Harold complained a little, but he eventually stopped. With small dietary changes, I was able to lower and maintain his pressure around 120 over 70, without the medication.

When it was time to eat, Harold could handle a knife and fork reasonably well. Sometimes he needed a little help cutting his steak or buttering his bread. Soup, on the other hand, was out of the question. The tremors in his hands were at the point where most of the soup would end up on his shirt. Sometimes he was shaking so much that he couldn't even finish writing his name. Therefore, at our next doctor's visit, we addressed this problem. The doctor prescribed a Parkinson's medication that he started taking twice a day. Over the next several months, I could see a definite improvement in Harold's signature, and he could finally use a spoon well enough to eat soup again. Following this doctor's visit, we had basically addressed most of Harold's medical problems.

During June of 2003, St. Anthony, which had been open for about one hundred twenty-five years, was going to hold its final mass. Attendance had slowly dwindled over the last decade, and financially the church could no longer afford to stay open. My father, dressed in a suit and tie as usual, attended the mass along with the rest of our family. After it was over, a reporter began interviewing him in the back of church. Harold said, "It's almost like losing a family member." My parents, one brother, and two sisters were all married at St. Anthony. My brothers, sisters, and I also attended grade school there. It was sad to see the doors close for the final time.

One friend of Harold's during World War II was a squad mate nicknamed Leebsey. They would often go on leave together to London and Paris. Harold had several wartime photos of the two of them, along with a few old brochures of where they went on leave. From what Harold said over the years, they were very good friends throughout the war. During the summer of 2004, Leebsey called our house one afternoon. Somehow he had tracked down my father and our phone number. The two of them hadn't talked for over forty years. At the time, I felt sorry for Harold. He wasn't in the best condition mentally, and the conversation didn't go very well. They talked for a little while, but it would have been nice to have my father in better shape to talk to his old friend.

Assisting Harold each day would start out around 10:45 a.m. He was not a very happy camper in the morning. I would quietly walk into his room and tell him it was time to get up. He'd lie there and complain a little, and then I would take some clean underwear, an undershirt, and his electric razor into the bathroom. I'd also put some toothpaste on his toothbrush. This way I could make sure he brushed his teeth. Harold did better when there were visual reminders of what he needed to do. Then, I'd head back into his room, and of course he was still lying there. One trick I found to get him out of bed was to stand there and stare at him. I don't think anyone can sleep with that going on. After a few minutes, he would look up at me, complain a little, and finally get up. As Harold got started in the bathroom, I would make his bed and set out his clothes for the day. I usually sat outside the bathroom and listened to make sure he washed up, shaved, and brushed his teeth. When it sounded like everything was going well, I would head down to the kitchen and get his breakfast started. About half an hour later, I'd head back upstairs, and Harold was usually close to finished in the bathroom. He had the nicest, silvery white hair. When he was nearly finished, I would go in and shampoo it over the sink. A quick run over with the hair dryer, and he was ready to go. I helped him get dressed, he combed his hair, and we went downstairs for his breakfast. I usually set out his pills on the kitchen table to make sure he took them. Sometimes he would sit down, look up at me, and say, "I've taken these pills already today." I could tell by his expression that he was serious, but this simply wasn't possible. On one occasion, his doctor wanted to prescribe a medication that he would take three times a day. I looked at the doctor and told him that wasn't going to work. Getting him to take pills once a day was hard enough. Harold didn't get much exercise, but after breakfast he and I would head down to the basement for his ten-minute stationary bike ride. He would complain about this also, but another trick that worked pretty well was turning on The Western Channel. It was like flipping a light switch. He was instantly happy riding the bike and watching television. When his ride was over, we would hurry upstairs, so he didn't miss much of the movie. Harold sat down in his recliner, and I'd get him a glass of ice water. He liked the western stars of the 1940s and '50s like Roy Rogers and Hopalong Cassidy, but his favorite was probably Gene Autry. Throughout his life, Harold enjoyed music, and Gene offered the best of both worlds, music and westerns. He was pretty content watching television, and repeats were never a problem. Sometimes, Harold and I would watch a western on one afternoon and the same one a few days later. I'd ask him, "Have you seen this movie before?" With a serious look, he usually replied, "No, I don't think so." Things did get a little tricky when it was time for dinner. Harold liked to eat at five o'clock in the evening and in his chair with a tray table. The problem was he became somewhat mesmerized by the westerns, and he wouldn't touch his dinner. I had to make sure any movie he watched ended close to five o'clock. I'd switch to the evening news, and Harold would concentrate on eating. When we did eat at home, I cooked about half the time, and we brought in carryout the other half. I made some of my mother's old recipes that he enjoyed. Over the years, Harold drank Coca-Cola, but with his mild diabetes, he couldn't handle all that sugar. Diet Pepsi was the next best option, so I would empty a can in a glass with some ice. He'd drink this with dinner, and if he asked, I said it was Coke. I didn't enjoy lying to him about this, but it made things a little easier. We would finish dinner around six o'clock, I'd clean up everything, and he continued watching television. After the dishes were finished, I usually went upstairs and messed around on the computer for an hour or so. Playing games was a great way for me to relieve stress. Around eight o'clock, I'd head back downstairs and join him watching television. Each night at eleven o'clock, we'd turn on British comedies on PBS. We switched between *Keeping Up Appearances* and *Are You Being Served?* He'd laugh through most of the show, and it put him in a good mood when it came time for bed. At half past eleven, we would head upstairs, and he'd get started in the bathroom. Prior to this, I'd put toothpaste on his toothbrush, so I could make sure he brushed his teeth. After Harold finished, I would help him on with his pajamas, and it was off to bed. During the night, if I heard him get up to go to the bathroom, I would also get up just to make sure everything was okay. This was our daily routine for about two years.

Occasionally in the afternoon, I would have to take Harold out for a haircut or to the bank. When I interrupted one of his movies, he was not very happy. For a few minutes he was almost furious, but when we'd sit down in the car, he was perfectly content. His mood swings were unpredictable and hard to deal with sometimes. Once Harold was out in public, he was usually pretty happy. He loved talking to people, and most of them were very patient with him. When he was getting his hair cut, Harold would sometimes ask his barber the same questions two and three times, but the barber didn't mind.

Harold tried to cover himself when he couldn't remember things, but you could see in his face that he was confused. Thankfully, he never got to the point where he didn't know who I was, and he never did wander off by himself.

During my twelve years at the bar I basically had no social life. I didn't mind it too much; however, I was always kind of a workaholic. While taking care of Harold, my social life was about the same. I tried going out a few times without him, but all I would do is worry, so what was the point? Watching him slowly deteriorate wasn't easy, but he had done so much for me over my life that it was time to return the favor. When he was younger, my father had to spend several years in a home for boys. I was determined not to let him end his life in a nursing home.

Things were very hard for the both of us. I remember asking God on a few occasions, "Please God, take one of us, and I don't care which one." I was obviously under enormous pressure during this period. Running my business was a piece of cake compared to being a caretaker.

After Eileen's husband, Bob, passed away in January of 1991, my mother called her about every day to talk. Bob and Eileen didn't have any children, and she was alone for the first time in decades, which I'm sure wasn't easy. After Martha passed away in August of 2000, I started calling Eileen every Sunday. We would talk for about an hour or so in the afternoon, and then Harold and I would head out for dinner. Occasionally I asked her if she wanted to join us, but she usually declined. As Harold's condition worsened over the coming years, my conversations with Eileen shifted to her mainly helping me with my current situation. She was a nurse by profession, so that helped, but her moral support was even more important. Over my life, I've slowly realized that where we are is exactly where we're supposed to be. I'm thankful that she was there for me.

One defining moment in my life occurred during a trip to the basement for Harold's daily exercise. He was in pretty bad shape at the time, physically, mentally, and emotionally. I was really frustrated and thought to myself, "Lord, what is he doing here?" A very loud voice in my head replied, "You are not here for his salvation, he is here for yours!" I was taken aback, and I didn't fully understand what this meant until later in my life.

As Harold's condition slowly got worse, the stress of wondering how much time he had left also bothered me. It felt like I was in a room with a ticking time bomb, and I had no idea when it was going off.

One evening in late January of 2005, I was upstairs on the computer for my nightly stress relief. About 7:30 p.m., I heard a loud crashing sound come from the living room. I rushed downstairs and Harold was on the floor, face up, and unconscious. From the look of the room, it appeared he fell pretty hard, hitting his head on the wall near the floor. Our older home had rock solid walls, and his head was bleeding a lot. I put a pillow under his head, tried to stop the bleeding, and held his hand. After a minute, he opened his eyes, and I asked him if he could hear me. He looked up at me and tried to speak, but couldn't. I knew it was serious, so I ran to the phone and dialed 911. The operator said an ambulance was on the way, so I propped open our front door and went back to holding Harold's hand. The paramedics arrived, and they wanted to get him to the hospital as soon as possible. When we arrived at the emergency room, he was conscious, but he still couldn't speak. Soon after, a nurse took him to run some tests, and when I saw him about an hour later, he was unconscious. They eventually put him in a room overnight, so I went home about one o'clock in the morning to try and get some sleep. Later that morning, I talked to the neurosurgeon, and the news wasn't good. He said that Harold hit his head in the worst possible area. He had a cerebral hemorrhage, and the doctor said with or without surgery, he probably wasn't going to make it.

The next few days were the roughest of my life. Harold remained unconscious the entire time. I would travel back and forth from the hospital twice a day, for about four hours each time. I could tell things weren't going very well. Even though he was on oxygen, his breathing was more shallow each visit.

Another defining moment in my life occurred on the last day of my father's life. On the third day Harold was in the hospital, a nurse called my sisters and me into his room. She said his breathing was very shallow and it wouldn't be much longer. About five minutes later he stopped breathing, and I noticed a drastic change in his appearance. As when my mother passed away, it just did not look like him anymore. A few seconds later a loud voice in my head said, *Everything is okay, Son.* I was stunned at that moment. During the last year, Harold would sometimes say, "What's for dinner, son?" or "What's on TV, Son?" I knew it was him speaking to me. Shortly after that, I was absolutely sure of life after death. This event was life changing for me, and it marked the beginning of my journey back to the Catholic faith. Prior to writing this book, I haven't told anyone about this. For a few years, I was always afraid of what people would think.

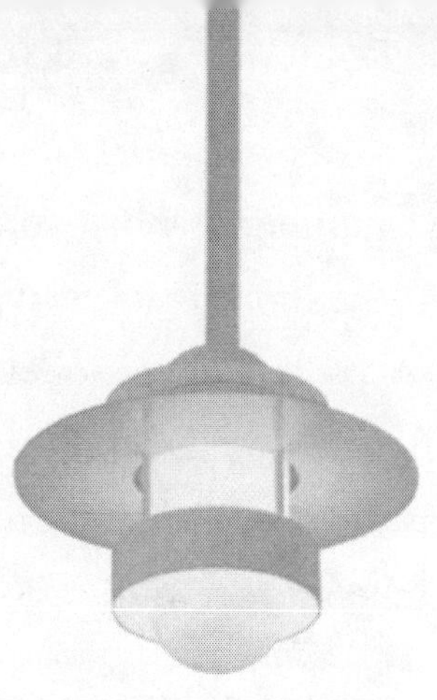

Trying to Figure Out Life

Trying to make sense of what happened when my father passed away and dealing with the fact that I felt alone for the first time in my life, I wasn't sure what direction to head into. For the last several years, taking care of Harold required my full attention, and now I had all this free time.

Throughout my life, I was never really obsessed with making money, but as a CPA, financial security was always number one or two on my priority list. During the months following my father's death, I was amazed at how money became less and less significant. Taking care of Harold for all those years was the hardest thing I had ever done, and it became the most rewarding.

Harold was born on January 6th, and I'm very thankful we could celebrate his eightieth birthday before he passed away. Fortunately our entire family was able to attend. We went to a fine dining restaurant for dinner then back to our house for cake, ice cream, and presents. He was like a little boy opening Christmas presents. I could tell he was very happy that everyone was there for him.

After Harold's death, Eileen and I started going out to dinner every Sunday. During one evening I told her, "You know, taking care of Harold was the hardest thing I had ever done, and it was sometimes unpleasant. Right now, though, I'm so thankful I did it. I wouldn't trade the last five years for a million dollars."

As far as our Wednesday night dinner club, Eileen, Pauline, and I decided to ask my sister-in-law, Deb, to join us. Deb's two children were grown up and out on their own at this time, so she didn't have much in the way of company. She agreed to join us and the four of us have been going out ever since.

One Saturday afternoon in March of 2008, I was watching *The Making of Rick Steves' Europe* on PBS. It basically showed how they produce each of his travel shows. Near the end, Rick explained that he occasionally ran into people traveling from the U.S. who watched his shows over the years. They usually talked for a little while, and sometimes Rick would use them in a cameo shot. I was sitting there, thinking it would be nice to see him one day and personally thank him. For the last few years of Harold's life, we couldn't travel, but we did enjoy watching Rick's shows. That following Wednesday, our monthly dinner group went out to celebrate Deb's birthday at a fine dining restaurant in Cincinnati. We arrived about 6:00 p.m., were seated at our table, and the evening was going very well. About half an hour later, a large party came in and sat down at the table next to us. At some point I glanced over, and there was someone sitting at the head of the table. I glanced back a little later and thought, "Boy, he looks familiar." Finally, I realized it was Rick Steves. I couldn't believe it! How high are the odds that four days later, a person who travels the world would be sitting next to me at the same restaurant and at the same time? Apparently he was in town for pledge week at our local PBS station. He was pretty busy, and I didn't want to interrupt his dinner, so I didn't get the chance to thank him for Harold and me. It was amazing

MICHAEL STIDHAM

72

that I had the chance to see him in person. Prior to this, I never would have thought it possible.

Martha worked her entire career at the same Salvation Army Hospital. In our area we also had a very large entertainment and supper club. It was very popular and brought in some high-quality entertainment from around the country. With several large rooms, it could easily hold about 3,000 people. One evening when I was eleven years old, Harold, Martha, and I were watching television, and the local channels broke in with an important news story. This was rarely done back in those days. A fire had developed inside the supper club, and the details were very sketchy. About twenty minutes later our phone rang, and it was the hospital where Martha worked. All of the hospitals in the area were calling in employees because the magnitude of the fire was getting worse. Martha had the worry of going in to work and seeing the injured, plus worrying about

Eileen and her husband, Bob. They were both at the supper club on this particular evening. No one had cell phones in those days, so it was impossible for us to know about their condition. Fortunately, several hours later we received a call that Bob and Eileen were all right. Over 150 people had lost their lives in the fire that night, with another 200 or so injured.

I was always a little upset with Harold's doctor after Bob passed away. I wondered what Harold's condition would have been if certain things were caught earlier. Eileen, however, continued going to her doctor friend up until he retired. She never had a bad word to say about him. I was always a little puzzled by this until one day when I asked her about him. Eileen told me that back when Bob and she were at the supper club on the night of the fire, a bus boy ran into their room and said, "There's a fire and you need to get out!" Most of the patrons were puzzled at first, and then he said, "This is no joke, get the hell out!" Everyone started moving to the exits, but somehow Bob and Eileen were separated. It was smoky and dark with everyone pushing and shoving. At one point Eileen was pushed to the ground and couldn't get up. The next thing she remembered was someone grabbing her by the arm, lifting her up, and saying, "Come on, Eileen, let's go." It was her doctor friend that she stuck by all those years. At that moment, I completely understood why she was so loyal to him. How could you possibly repay someone for saving your life?

One day I was watching an episode of *Rome Reports* on EWTN. A doctor was being interviewed in Africa, and he was expressing thanks for a certain medication he could administer to the local population. One comment he made I found very interesting. He basically said that having the medication was nice, but it wouldn't work very well because the population suffered from poor nutrition. I thought this was very insightful. After all, my car won't run very well with dirty oil and bad gasoline, so why wouldn't our bodies operate in the same way? When I was working between 2000 and 2002, I often worried about whether Harold was eating properly. Most of the time I was working from nine o'clock in the morning to eight o'clock at night, so I couldn't keep an eye on his eating habits. I sometimes wonder if his diet during those years didn't affect his condition. Fortunately after 2002, I could make sure he ate properly and regularly.

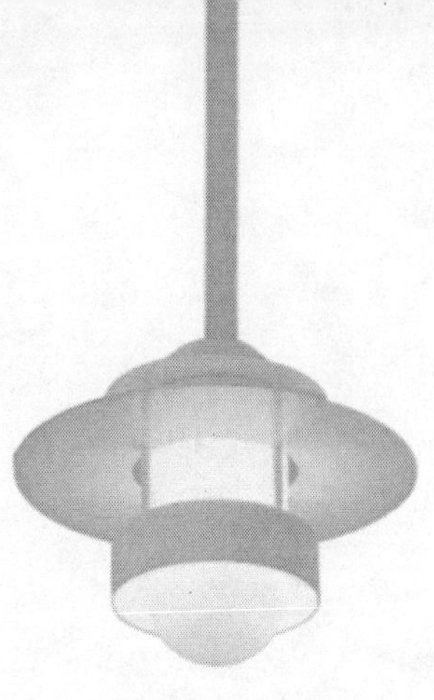

My Spiritual Awakening

For most of my life, I was somewhat of a control freak. The best analogy I can offer is riding in a two-person canoe down the river of life. I'm in the front, with the only oar, and God is sitting in the back. As time went on, I kept trying to control things by steering left and right, sometimes even working against the current. Occasionally it was a futile effort. For the longest time, I let God sit in the back of the canoe with his arms folded.

How crazy was that? A few years ago I decided to hand God the oar and let him do the steering. After all, God has a plan for everyone, including myself. But just because things are planned out, don't assume life's going to be boring. Mine certainly hasn't been.

One evening, I was channel surfing on television and ran across someone who looked familiar. He reminded me of a fireman I knew from my sports bar. The show was on EWTN, and the host was Father John Corapi. I decided to watch for a little while and listen to what he had to say. I've been watching him regularly now since May of 2005. Earlier in my life I would have never thought it possible that I would be sitting there watching a religious program for a few hours a week. I was no longer the teenager that thought he knew everything. It's amazing how much he's helped me put the pieces of my life's puzzle together.

One day while watching Father Corapi, he asked, "Do you know what the worst and the best thing that ever happened was?" I had no idea. He said, "Jesus being crucified on the cross." It was the worst thing because Jesus, through his human nature, suffered and died on the cross. But it was also the best thing because Jesus paved the way for all of us to go to heaven. He explained that this was the paradox of the cross. For me this really brought into focus how something good could come out of a bad event in life. This helped me further understand the period when I was taking care of Harold. It was the hardest thing I had ever done, but it also became the most rewarding. I still find this paradox fascinating.

Another concept that has helped me immensely concerns how God feels about each and every one of us. God loves the sinner, but not the sin. It is *extremely* important that you learn how to separate the two. For the longest time, I didn't understand this concept. I would look at someone who wasn't living the best moral life and think ill of them. We're all basically prone to sin through our human nature. You and I must love our relatives and neighbors. We don't, however, have to love the sin that is eating away at their souls.

I look back at my clients, most of whom were very good people, and I sometimes think of the sports bar as "the island of lost souls." They were all looking for happiness, and there's nothing wrong with that. Most of them, however, were looking for material possessions to make them happy. For a short term, those things might work, but to be truly happy in the long run, you've got to allow God in your life. If you have all the possessions in the world, but you don't allow God in your life, then you've got nothing!

One of my regular clients at the sports bar was named Ray. He looked somewhat like Santa

Claus except with a shorter beard and hair. He was the wisest man I knew, with the least formal education. I always found that fascinating. He was the first regular customer I can remember, and he remained there until the end. I learned many things over the years from him, including the following. Two customers of mine were father and son. Both had separately bid on several heating and air-conditioning jobs in the area. Concerning one job, the father had won the contract, and his son was furious. Ray turned to me and said, "Can you believe that? He should be happy that his father got the work!" I myself would not have gotten mad, but it wasn't until later in life that I fully understood what Ray meant. If you truly love your family, you should be happy for their good fortune, not jealous because they've got something you don't have.

Over time, as I watched the older television shows with Harold, I noticed a major contrast from today's programming. Back then, Hopalong Cassidy, for example, portrayed kind of a virtuous father figure. I recalled something Ray once said to me, "We need a hero bad. The kids today are growing up without one." He was right. Fifty years ago, they had several. Hopalong Cassidy and the other western stars portrayed a good, moral character base for children to follow. Most of today's programming centers on graphic violence. After all, the reason someone watches television is to be entertained. How can murder and rape be entertaining? It's amazing how desensitized I became over the years. It's no wonder children today are shooting up their high schools, using drugs, and committing suicide. Murder and other violent crimes shown on television are perceived as normal behavior, when nothing could be further from the truth.

During one of his lectures, Father Corapi discussed the importance of humility. The closest definition I can offer is that humility is the opposite of arrogance. Ultimately, God wants you in heaven, and among other things, you've got to learn humility. You can either learn it on your own, or if you're *falling behind in class,* God can teach it to you. Most people learn through the latter as I did, during a difficult life experience (redemptive suffering). To watch my father, a once-vibrant man, slowly turn into an empty shell of a human being was very humbling for me.

The theological definition of humility is the acknowledgement of the truth. It is the proclamation of who God is and who I am. God is God, the creator, the all powerful one. All seeing, all knowing, and all present. Who am I? I'm the creature. I'm a speck of dust in the universe, but God loves the speck. That is humility. That is the truth. Pride, or arrogance, is just a lie.

If you're not sure how to start on the road

to humility, try putting God first, everyone else second, and yourself last. After all, Jesus said, "I come to serve, not to be served." Humility is an absolute prerequisite for holiness. It is the gem casket of all virtues. No humility, no holiness. No holiness, no heaven! This doesn't mean you have run out on day one and build a homeless shelter. Start out small, and work your way up. Hold the door for someone or let someone go ahead of you in traffic. You'll be amazed at the good things that start to happen. We all have to work our way into heaven, and God isn't going to care about your checking account balance. What you do for your neighbor in life holds a lot more weight than the goods you accumulate. Fortunately today, I have a much clearer view of the people around me. There, but for the grace of God, go I. I could be that homeless person living under that bridge. As far as humility goes, I always consider myself a work in progress.

God wants us to love him by choice, that's why he gave us a free will. Eternal life or eternal death, good or evil, the choice is yours. The simple fact is that we are in a constant state of spiritual combat. Good versus evil. I'm not making this up. Saint Paul talked about spiritual combat 2,000 years ago. In any war you've got to know whom the enemy is. The devil's greatest weapon is for you to think he doesn't exist. In this way he can operate freely and out in the open. Once you realize who the enemy is, you've made a major, first step because the devil's primary focus is attacking your family. Divide and conquer. The devil is a patient opportunist that knows our weaknesses and takes advantage of them when he can. The sad reality is that the devil wants you, your children, and your family to end up lying dead in a garbage can. That being said, all is not lost, so please don't panic.

In any war you have to know about your

weapons and tactics, as well as your enemy's. It's the same with spiritual combat. Fortunately we have great weapons at our disposal. Humility and prayer are two that are of vital importance. How can the devil possibly tempt one who is humble? He is powerless to do so. From time to time, if you're running low on humility as I do, pray for a refill. If your family members are stumbling into sin, pray for them. We are all soldiers in God's army, and sin is a wound that we receive on the battlefield. I look back at my twelve years at the bar and realize I was observing the front lines of spiritual combat.

In January of 2006, after a twenty-five-year absence, I started regularly praying again. At first, I was embarrassed because I could barely remember the words to the "Our Father" and the "Hail Mary." In the beginning, I started each day with one "Hail Mary" and one "Our Father." Since then, I've worked my way up to five decades of the rosary a day and continue upward.

For the longest time, I was a little puzzled about part of the "Our Father." Near the end it says, "…as we forgive those who trespass against us, *lead us not* into temptation…" I never understood why a good and loving God would lead us into temptation in the first place. Unfortunately as you translate from one language to another, the meaning of what you translate can become distorted. During one lecture, Father Corapi explained that he preferred a Spanish version of the "Our Father." In this version, the section I was confused about reads, "…as we forgive those who trespass against us, *let us not* fall into temptation…" Praying to God for help avoiding temptation makes much more sense to me.

One of my favorite stories from Father Corapi concerns a young couple about to get married in the Catholic Church. A local pastor asked him to sit down and talk with them. When the couple arrived for their meeting with the lovable parish priest, they found Father Corapi waiting instead. During the meeting he asked the groom, "So what do you want for your future wife?" He replied, "Well I'd like a nice house for us, a nice car, financial security." Father Corapi replied, "Well those are all good things; anything else?" The groom replied, "Well, I don't think so." Then he asked the bride what she wanted for her future husband. She replied, "Well, maybe children, early retirement." Then he asked her, "Anything else?" She replied, "I don't think so." Then Father Corapi hit them with the punch line. "What about heaven?" If you love someone, you should want the very best for them and that includes doing anything and everything to get them into heaven. This was very eye opening for me. Ultimately there are only two choices, heaven or hell. How could I possibly want anything but to eventually see my relatives and friends in heaven? This is one reason why I pray for them and myself every day.

God is the best friend you'll ever have. Don't be afraid to pray and ask him to help you, your family members, or who ever you feel needs it. I don't care if you only start with one "Our Father" a day. Even the longest journey requires you to take the first step.

If you're under the opinion that God couldn't possibly forgive what you have done in the past, please put that aside. For it is actually a form of arrogance to assume that your sins are greater than God's mercy. This is simply not true.

One doctrine of the Catholic faith concerns the angels and the fact that they are real. There are good angels and also the fallen angels, the devil and his minions. The term angel means *messenger*. The good angels are messengers from us to God, via our prayers, and sometimes vise versa. When Father Corapi explained this during one of his lectures, I was awestruck. Several events in my life fell right into place. What I heard on the way to Harold's daily exercise ("You are not here for his salvation, he is here for yours!") and what I had heard immediately after Harold's death ("Everything is okay, son.") all came into focus. My life hasn't been the same since. I'm absolutely convinced that angels do exist and that there is life after death.

Finally, I'd like to say that I have a very deep respect for those of you taking care of your children, caring for an elderly relative, and especially those of you taking care of someone with Alzheimer's. I know it's not easy, but you sacrifice every day, and I just want you to know that God appreciates everything you do out of love. For you cannot have authentic love without sacrifice. Life is far from easy, but there is light at the end of the tunnel. One day in the not-too-distant future, you will be standing before God. He will smile

at you and say, "Well done, my good and faith-
ful servant. Enter into the joy of your master's
house." May God bless you.

---

listen|imagine|view|experience

AUDIO BOOK DOWNLOAD INCLUDED WITH THIS BOOK!

In your hands you hold a complete digital entertainment package. Besides purchasing the paper version of this book, this book includes a free download of the audio version of this book. Simply use the code listed below when visiting our website. Once downloaded to your computer, you can listen to the book through your computer's speakers, burn it to an audio CD or save the file to your portable music device (such as Apple's popular iPod) and listen on the go!

How to get your free audio book digital download:

1. Visit www.tatepublishing.com and click on the e|LIVE logo on the home page.
2. Enter the following coupon code:
   837d-0f2f-7ec4-5076-69fa-fad4-ce96-b214

   Download the audio book from your e|LIVE digital locker and begin enjoying your new digital entertainment package today!